THE GREEN SHOOTS OF MONEY
LET'S GET GOING!

Ian Moncrief-Scott

Information Management Solutions Limited

ISLE OF MAN

The author Ian Moncrief-Scott has asserted his right under the Copyright, Designs and Patents Act 1988 to be identified as the author of this work.

Copyright. © I. Moncrief-Scott 2021

All rights reserved. No part of this publication may be produced in any form or by any means - graphic, electronic, or mechanical, including photocopying, recording, taping, or information storage and retrieval systems - without the prior permission in writing of the publishers.

The publishers make no representation, express or implied, regarding the accuracy of the information contained in this book and cannot accept any legal responsibility for any errors or omissions that may take place.

A CIP catalogue record for this book is available from the British Library.

Published by Information Management Solutions Limited, 17 Howe Road, Onchan, Isle of Man, IM3 2BB.

Printed, bound and distributed by IngramSpark.

Book Layout © 2017 BookDesignTemplates.com

Cover design by Tanja Prokop of BookDesignTemplates.com

Superhero Peg Image: Besjunior/Shutterstock.com

THE GREEN SHOOTS OF MONEY: LET'S GET GOING! – 1st ed.
ISBN 9781903467107

The Publishers have been requested by the author to acknowledge the direct and indirect contributions to this book by:

The Bank of England
Bank of England Museum
Mr David Sinclair
Daily Mail Newspapers
De La Rue PLC
European Monetary Institute
European Central Bank
American Museum of Finance
The Rothschild Archive
International Bond & Share Society

This book is dedicated to
start-up entrepreneurs.

The front cover depicts
ordinary wooden clothes pegs dressed as
Super Heroes.

**All start-up entrepreneurs are
ordinary people
turning into Super Heroes!**

CONTENTS

THE ETERNAL OLD LADY 1
DE LA RUE STRAW HATS TO SECURITIES 9
CURRANTS, OLIVES & COTTON 21
TAIL-LESS CATS & THREE-LEGGED MEN 31
THE EURO 35
AS GOOD AS GOLD - THE HISTORY OF STERLING 41
SCRIPOPHILY 47
BIBLIOGRAPHY 57
OTHER BOOKS BY THE AUTHOR 59
FORTHCOMING BOOKS BY THE AUTHOR 61

CHAPTER ONE

THE ETERNAL OLD LADY

War created the Bank of England.

Had King William III possessed enough money to combat France's Louis X1V, the first public bank may have never emerged. According to his statue in the magnificent Hall of the Bank, the King is credited with founding the formidable institution, but a commoner,

William Paterson first conceived the Old Lady.

With a more trusted Government, a less reckless previous monarch and properly accounted state money, the Bank would have been unimaginable.

Money lending was ancient. Discounting bills of exchange went back to the 12th century.

In London, goldsmiths paid interest on deposits. Scriveners (solicitors' mortgage clerks) raised funds. Merchants, brokers, usurers and discounters of bills and tallies operated routinely. Joint Stock Companies like Sword Mills Company and Mine Adventurers issued notes and lent money on securities.

These independent activities converged with cheque payments between 1830-1870. Note issue was the last classical banking function to evolve in England and contributed significantly to today's European banking system.

City of London Bank failed in 1682. National Bank of Credit folded a year later. Daring proposals were needed for a public bank.

In 1687, the first treasure was salvaged from a Spanish ship lost 40 years earlier in Hispaniola. Investors returned 10,000% profit -20% of the entire national revenue. Despite war by the Grand Alliance against France, over 150 treasure hunting companies and the new stock exchange inspired an economic miracle.

Ironically, William Paterson was a Scot. Born in Dumfriesshire, he travelled to America to seek his fate. Some say he became a buccaneer, others a missionary. Fact reveals that he worked for London's Merchant Tailors Company. He journeyed to the West Indies and visited both Hamburg and Amsterdam, two pinnacles of banking.

Paterson formed a company in 1691 to lend His Majesty's Government £1 million at 6% annual interest with a £5000 management fee. The offer was rejected. His second proposal, a £2 million loan, was similarly scorned.

Charles Montagu tried to fill the Exchequer void with a Lottery loan. It failed miserably. Paterson was again invited. This time, powerful Whig merchants and the City of London supported the venture.

Paterson, also noted for the flawed Darien Adventure, an attempt to colonise the Panama Isthmus that gorged half of Scotland's wealth was joined by Sir John Houblon, a subsequent Lord Mayor of London.

Dr Nicholas Borbon, an insurance magnate and son of landbank advocate, Praisegod 'Barebones' and John Holland, a reputable Englishman who promoted the Bank of Scotland, added their support.

Subscription (25% paid up) was launched on June 21 at Mercers' Hall, Cheapside. It was swift. £900,000 arrived within the first four days, the balance by the twelfth. Wealthy Whig merchants from the City seized the opportunity. Even the King and Queen, through the Treasury Office, committed £10,000.

Investors included treasure seekers and companies from the diverse fields of paper, linen, copper, glass, water and mining. Even, 'The Society for Improving Native Manufacture so as to keep out the Wet' and the 'Company for Sucking-Worm Engines of Mr John Lofttingh' (fire hoses) joined the euphoria.

Opposition had festered throughout the campaign. Tories demanded a competitor bank to protect the country from the predicted wave of socialism the Bank would create. Whig politicians had misgivings that the Crown might again seize control of the funds without the will of Parliament.

For years, the Stuart Kings, James & Charles had ruthlessly manipulated the nation's funds.

Assent for The Bank of England Charter emerged on 27 July 1694. In Grocers' Hall, the Old Lady, manifested by Britannia beside a mound of money, was born. She would remain there until 1734 before finally moving to Threadneedle Street. Sir John Houblon, head of a leading shipping and trading firm, became the first governor and with his deputy, Michael Godfrey, led 24 directors.

Official records show both men to be 'grocers'.

Two clauses of the Charter reflected the mood of the day. No Crown lending without Parliament's approval and no goods trading, except bills of exchange and gold and silver. The former prohibited a repeat of Stuart misappropriations and the latter pampered the jealousy of the City merchants.

A Tory Land Bank was finally promoted. Six months later, in 1696, the protege crashed and the Bank of England was finally placed to assume a mighty position.

The Charter allowed the Bank to circulate notes to the value of its capital which, at the time, was lent entirely to the Government. An overlooked clause permitted cheques, obscure Dutch devices, which were later to revolutionise banking and proliferate a plethora of country banks.

Early notes were handwritten. They could be cashed in part and endorsed 'encashable' without time limit. Two centuries later, a man produced a note for cashing and asked to keep the item as a souvenir. He was promptly told that it became the property of the Bank and so he left one penny outstanding to gain his souvenir.

Within two years a huge shock rocked the Bank. Coins from gunmetal, iron and silvered copper, damaged over time and heavily clipped, were to be withdrawn. Old coins, valued by weight, would be replaced by a new mint of face value. The Bank would lose half its money. Calling up 50% of its unpaid capital to 80%, just saved the day.

The crisis subsided, but several more loomed large.

Using salt duties for the forthcoming year as security, the Government in 1697 encouraged the Bank to raise yet more cash. This time for war in Flanders. In return for the £1,001,171 at 8% interest, the Bank of England gained a monopoly.

The famous Clause 28 declared 'no Corporation, Society, Fellowship, Company or Constitution in the nature of a bank was to be erected or established, permitted, suffered, countenanced, nor allowed during the continuance of the Bank of England'.

Anyone caught forging the Bank's currency would be sentenced to death, 'without the benefit of clergy', an exact penalty as existed for clipping or coining the King's money.

The Bank had obtained the approval of the Realm.

Though it now had a unique role, the Old Lady made an enormous mistake in not opening branches and offering countrywide access to capital. Total control of the banking business was there for the taking.

In 1707, the Government under The Act of Union, with Scotland appointed the Bank as fiscal agent for Exchequer Bills worth £1.5 million and initiated the close Treasury ties that exist today.

To prevent Joint Stock Companies encroaching the Bank's privileged Charter, an Act in 1708 prohibited any entity with more than six partners from issuing notes, payable on demand in less than six months. Though successfully frustrating opposition, it did lead to numerous small traders conducting banking business, only frequently to fail though over-ambition and recklessness.

Renewal of the Charter approached again. A South Seas frenzy and another war, with Spain this time, spawned dubious flotations. 'Salt pans for Holy Island.' 'A Wheel for Perpetual Motion.' 'A machine gun that fires round and square ammunition, round for Christian enemies-square for Turks.' 'An Undertaking of Great Advantage-which will be revealed in due course.'

The Bubble burst.

Sword Blade Bank went bust in 1712 and there was a run on the Old Lady. To stem the flow, the staff made payments in sixpences and shillings to friends who carried them round to the Bank's back door to enable the tills to be replenished.

When Bonnie Prince Charlie threatened to return with a French invasion force, it caused the first Black Friday, 6 December 1745.

Once more the coin mechanism of the employees was seen to work.

In reality, merchants meeting at Garraways Coffee House in Change Alley, Lombard Street, the future home of Barclays

Bank Plc saved the situation. They resolved to accept banknotes and use them for payment themselves.

A crushing battle at Culloden ended the Prince's aspirations. The '45 crisis abated.

In 1780, The Old Lady was nearly stormed during the Gordon Riots. 534 soldiers were despatched to defend her honour.

After the Lord Major was pushed to the ground, the Bank threatened 'if this 'arrogant behaviour persisted' it would leave Threadneedle Street for the safety of Somerset House.

She never did. She stayed steadfast in the heart of the City of London to develop, arguably, the most envied and admired reputation in the world today.

CHAPTER TWO

DE LA RUE
STRAW HATS TO SECURITIES

While other Guernseymen prospered from privateering in the English Channel, fortune did not bless the household De La Rue. Nine children had depleted Eleazer's resources. His son, Thomas, had arrived as Madam Guillotine severed the reign of King Louis XVI.

It was 1793.

After his apprenticeship, the young Thomas tasted printing with the 'Publiciste' newspaper before publishing his own 'Miroir Politique.' But like Dick Wittington, aged 25, he headed for London.

Waterloo had left England in a deep depression. The monarch was mad. Much reform was needed. Uncomfortable with the idea of printing in the competitive capital and high newspaper taxes, Thomas ventured into straw hat making.

Traditionally, beavers provided the substrate for bonnets. America had temporarily offset the shortage that had swept

Europe, but the 1812-14 war cut supplies. Thomas vigorously pursued success. Recounting his printing experience, he experimented with paper bonnets, under a French patent, using waterproofing and colour.

By 1824, embossed bookbinding attracted his attention and he formed a stationery partnership with Samuel Cornish and William Frederick Rock in 1830. As 'Cardmakers, Hot Pressers and Enamellers', they operated from Queen Street, Finsbury.

Bibliomania was sweeping London.

In 1829 Thomas and Mr. Balne of Gracechurch Street published a large royal edition of the New Testament, using gold powder for special copies. Later editions in 1834 and 1836 ensured De La Rue became deluxe.

Thomas was now synonymous with quality!

Meanwhile, Paul, his youngest brother, had joined the firm, now 'Wholesale Dealers in Leghorns, Chops and Straws'. The years 1831 and 1832 were significant for Thomas. De La Rue's first playing card was registered at Somerset House. 'His present most Excellent Majesty King William IV', granted a Royal Letters Patent for 'Certain Improvements in Making or Manufacturing and Ornamenting Playing Cards.'

Until then, cards had been hand-stencilled with watercolours or printed in one colour and hand-tinted. A costly, tedious and inexact process. Imagine trying hand colour fifty-two matched cards.

With innovation in mind, Thomas animated the wooden characters and revolutionised the reverse of the cards. He was soon 'the father of the English playing card and visiting card'.

Some called him the inventor of modern English colour printing, after patenting 'For Improvements in Producing Coloured Steel Plate, Copper Plate and Other Impressions'.

Bunhill Row's notable address appeared in 1834. It housed the new partnership of De La Rue, James and Rudd, 'Cardmakers, Embossers and Wholesale Fancy Stationers'. Thomas enlisted his son Warren, whose scientific paper on the Daniell electric battery led to electro-plating in typography, revolutionising security printing.

Times became difficult for the nation in 1837. On 26 May, long before public limited companies, Thomas was arrested for debt.

His old partnership dissolved, with new associates Fry and Nathan, he resolved to put matters in order. 1838 was make or break. De La Rue's ingenuity, his white lead patent and an £8500 loan from Mr. Charles Button, a wealthy chemist and chemical equipment importer, ensured a positive outcome.

On 28 June 1838, to celebrate Queen Victoria's coronation, he printed the Sun newspaper in gold. It sold out.

His innovation and foresight excelled. In 1840, he registered, 'Improvements in printing calicoes and surfaces'. This invention, using the Jacquard wire loom, enabled tartan-check patterns.

Post Office envelopes arrived in 1839. Previously, writing paper had been folded, sealed and the address written on the reverse. Security was poor.

A year later, Rowland Hill's prepaid Penny Postage scheme, with standard charges and regular deliveries, catapulted the Victorian propensity to correspond. By the decade's end, one million letters a day were being sent.

Aged 23, Warren supervised the 'erection of some large white lead works, the drawings for which he made himself entirely'. He also invented a special boiler, 'so constructed that the fine aroma of the tea was not lost'.

By 1832, The Duke of Wellington had established a railway. Cautiously remarking that this 'enabled the lower classes to travel about needlessly.'

De la Rue won its first order of railway tickets from the London Blackwall Railway in 1841. By 1846 the Company was making tickets for almost all railways in the UK. Within ten years, it was producing 1.5 million per week.

Thomas was introduced to the Tsar of all the Russias Court in 1843. He and Paul were so proficient that within four years, the Tsar's playing cards production multiplied from one to four million packs annually, becoming the world's largest manufacturer.

In St. Peterburg, Paul became friendly with the Winans, from Baltimore, USA, who were building the Trans-Siberian Railway. Eventually, Paul's daughter, Maria Ann, married Walter, son of millionaire Ross Winans. Though living in the

North, he was suspected of potentially delivering his extensive rolling-stock to the Confederacy and was imprisoned twice.

These relationships helped William Frederick obtain the famous Confederate stamp orders from Major Ben F Ficklin. The Five Cent Blue, with Jefferson Davies and the One Cent Orange, bearing John C Calhoun's head, were designed by Joubert de la Ferte.

The initial order was successfully delivered to Wilmington by the blockade runner Robert E Lee. Other consignments created the notorious Mercedita and Bermuda incidents.

However, De La Rue still opened its New York office a decade before the one in Paris.

Partners were being changed back in Bunhill Row. Button, the last outsider, departed in 1844 satisfied that Warren was now established. The firm now specialised in the fancy Victorian stationery, though until 1856, playing cards remained the core business.

After volunteering for the 4th Tower Hamlets, William Frederick became known as 'Colonel Billy'. Warren moved impressively in scientific circles, especially astronomy and lunar photography. His advice was increasingly sought on matters of commerce.

Both he and Thomas were heavily involved in the 1851 Great Exhibition at the Crystal Palace, the 1853 New York and the 1855 Paris Expositions.

April 1853 saw the Board of Inland Revenue move to employ adhesive fiscal stamps on drafts and receipts. De La Rue's improved typographical, or surface printing, vanquished all competition.

The Company started printing stamps for the East India Company. To strengthen its expertise, Dr. Hugo Muller, a Bavarian, was added to the staff. He perfected 'fugitive inks', a vital security feature that prevented cancellation marks from being erased for re-use.

In 1857 Colonel Billy overhauled Bunhill Row. The business had mushroomed and a plan was needed. To coax staff to drink tea instead of beer, Warren and Colonel Billy promoted a Tea Society.

Although the Company had a presence in India, Perkins Bacon, through the Crown Agents, dominated colonial stamps. Despite having only produced a small order for Ceylon, De La Rue capitalised on a mistake by Perkins Bacon. Colonel Billy's close relationship with the new Crown appointee Penrose Julyan clinched all the business.

With no experience of banknotes either, De La Rue was awarded the prestigious Mauritian £5, £1, & 10/- notes, the first of 109 issues made for various countries.

Long term printing contracts flowed. All Indian postage stamps ensued for 71 years, Ceylon 73 years, Great Britain 55 years. Lasting alliances with Italy, Ecuador, Uruguay, and Portugal developed.

Improving all the time, Thomas patented the two-colour process and better watermarking. Between 1857 and 1868, railway ticket output doubled, playing cards reached 265,000 packs.

Sadly, in 1866 aged 74, Thomas died and was buried in the fashionable Kensal Green cemetery.

Tragically, four years later, liver cancer struck 47-year-old Colonel Billy, then also Chairman of Eagle Star Insurance. His passing left the company unsettled.

Warren engaged his sons, Thomas Andros and Warren William. Quality stationery maintained its prestige, the copyright notepaper 'Imperial Treasury' and 'Fine Old Turkey Mill' were hugely popular. Warren's third son, Ernest, contributed ideas for firelighters, pocketbooks and bookmarkers.

In March 1877, the Globe newspaper heavily criticised Perkins Bacon, whose stamp contract was expiring, stating that De La Rue's receipt stamp was far better. The firm's moment to seize superiority had arrived.

Its letterpress technology and international experience won the new Penny Stamp contract.

From November 1879 to June 1881, the company made almost 1.5 billion One Penny stamps alone. Three new printing works were built, the Crown, George and Star. The future was glowing.

Something peculiar happened in April 1897, two years before Warren died. Nigeria complained about De La Rue stamps. Others followed, complaining the gumming was unsatisfactory.

The British Board of the Inland Revenue was emphatic in its support for the Company against Colonial attack. No further complaints were made, such was the pre-eminence.

Young Warren committed suicide. Although now a public company, the family and its friends still owned nearly all the shares. Thomas Andros ruled as a dictator.

Unexpectedly, Uganda rejected new designs, in preference to Waterlow & Sons copperplate-printed examples.

The writing was on the wall.

Thomas Andros's three sons arrived, Evelyn, noted for his 'Onoto' fountain pen invention, Ivor and Stuart. Edwardian days rolled comfortably on. All were blissfully unaware of impending disaster.

During 1911 the Inland Revenue proposed to divide its contract, awarding the higher denominations to De La Rue and the lower (more profitable) ones to Harrisons, which had never printed a stamp. In a fit of arrogant pique, Thomas Andros refused to share the contract. It was lost forever. He died some months later.

The outbreak of the Great War brought a brief respite. HM Treasury fearing a run on gold, gave the company an order for 2.5 million 10/- Treasury Notes. Waterlow Brothers and Layton (WB&L) printed the £1 denomination.

The second edition order was reversed after Stuart made a fuss. De La Rue printed all £1 sharing the 10/- notes with WB&L.

Later in the war, the Government realised that security improvement was needed to prevent forgery. De la Rue and Waterlow & Sons (not WB&L) conspired to defeat competition by a convenient tacit agreement.

To their mutual annoyance, the entire contract went to WB&L because of its new cheaper photogravure process.

With Thomas Andros and Evelyn in the army, Stuart was in sole charge. He was a hapless businessman. While other producers prospered during the war, the company reversed a £90,000 profit into a £90,000 loss.

Though De La Rue was struggling, some key Waterlow & Sons staff joined the company, bringing design, engraving and engineering photogravure expertise. Stuart left the firm after the competition conspiracy scandal emerged, ending the family reign.

Company affairs were again in disorder. Fifty-year-old machinery appeared in the books at full value.

Coincidently, the next day the Siamese Government wrote advising they wanted new currency. Bernard Westall was immediately despatched to prepare a tender.

While awaiting the outcome, he learned that Government was encountering forged customs certificates.

Westall knew Prince Viwat, a Cambridge contemporary, working in the Customs House and convinced him to introduce a De La Rue security device into customs forms.

The five-year banknote order was also secured.

A Spanish Government bond contract quickly followed.

Life was being breathed into the business. Overseas, salesmen Peter Loopuyt and Albert Avramov were appointed.

Acting for the American Banknote Company, the latter had beaten Waterlow & Sons to a Bulgarian order by bribing the Finance Minister. While Avramov escaped on the Simplon Express, the Minister was not so lucky. He was hanged for corruption.

Between Loopuyt and Avarmov, extensive banknote and stamp contracts flowed, including four billion postage stamps for China. Even the playing cards improved. 1932 provided a timely centenary for Thomas's 1832 patent for 'Improvements to Playing Cards'.

To emphasise the Company's metamorphosis and ensure foreign Finance Ministers never again doubted its stability, Westall launched the famous Annual Dinners. These were a resounding success and the guest list read like the United Nations Assembly.

Substantial Chinese business was secured. At £3 million, the largest order in the Company's history was snatched from ABC's grasp. De La Rue was back and would surge into the world's largest securities producer.

Having swallowed rivals Bradbury Wilkinson, Waterlow & Sons, Harrison and papermakers Portals, today De La Rue manufactures most facets of the money business.

From ATMs, coins, credit cards, smartcards, and passports to software, holograms, cheques, stamps, banknotes, and bonds worldwide.

Not a bad achievement for a straw hat maker from Guernsey.

CHAPTER THREE

CURRANTS, OLIVES & COTTON

Languishing in the azure Mediterranean Sea, the picturesque Ionian Isles seem an unlikely venue for vast international trade and the spread of Mexican dollars.

Undoubtedly, early links with Venice helped, but the influences of France, Turkey, Britain and, ultimately, Greece have left indelible marks.

In 1814, occupying French forces abandoned Corfu. Soon after the Napoleonic collapse, Ionia found itself hosting a 'protector', a Lord High Commissioner, courtesy of Great Britain.

Currants and olive oil provided an economic backbone. Currency was mainly coin, comprising silver dollars and Mexican and Maria Theresa thalers.

By 1825 Britain sought to determine Sterling as the unifying standard.

Credit hardly existed in this agricultural community. Poor, unorganised peasants suffered harshly under the dominance of monopolistic merchants. Meagre loans demanded usurious interest.

A cash society created other problems. Lord Nugent, The High Commissioner, remarked, "the keeping and secreting in private houses numerous and sometimes vast amounts of specie, which occasioned frequent predatory and frightful incursions from the Barbarians of Albania.

Commodity prices plummeted in the early 1830s through the Gold Standard's return, creating massive deflation. Former French occupiers had wreaked a legacy of havoc on indigenous output by squandering huge swathes of life-preserving olive groves and currant bushes for firewood. 25-30% interest rates were commonplace.

Farmers neared ruin.

Lord Nugent had a plan. Gold and silver hoards must be enticed into the open. He established a £35,000 fund with an interest rate of 6% for farming loans ahead of harvest. It was a huge success, much to the chagrin of merchants and moneylenders.

Inspired, he pursued the notion of a national fund and even local paper currency. It would stimulate the movement of capital and safely reward the Treasury.

Sadly, London scorned the concept.

The Lords Commissioners declared it "would most particularly and decidedly object to a British Government being considered in many ways responsible for any description of paper currency issued by the Government of the Ionian Islands" Lord Nugent resigned.

Mindful of his predecessor's mistakes, Sir Howard Douglas assumed the reins of power. He abandoned the national loan scheme and was careful not to be drawn into the rows.

Eventually, life on the Island mellowed his demeanour. Sir Douglas issued the vital recommendation for a United Ionian States Bank with powers for agricultural loans, pawnbroking and deposit-taking.

This time, London was more responsive. Perhaps, competitive threats of proposed Gibraltar and Malta Banks helped?

Subscription of four thousand £25 shares was planned for Island launch in 1837. Local Government would hold one-sixth, in return for a proportionate right to appoint directors. The response was poor.

Immediately, the project died.

The revival was equally swift. London became the focus of capital search. Ionian States London Agent, Sir Alexander Wood, formulated proposals for the Ionian State Bank.

Start-up capital was again £100,000 in £25 shares and the Bank was to be prescribed under Ionian State law with limited Ionian liability.

Key was the growing trade with Britain. "The Ionian Islands are so advantageously situated with respect to the Mediterranean, the Adriatic and the Levant, that the operations of the Bank are capable of easy and advantageous extension over a wide range, and thus the project established may be the nucleus of a great and important undertaking," heralded the glowing prospectus.

New offices at Aldermanbury, London, quickly bore the Minute Book's first entry. 1 March 1839, "the sum of £14,000 was lent to Messrs. John Wright & Co., Bankers, at 5% on the security of Florida Bonds, the loan subject to the call for payment at a fortnight's notice."

Later that month, two envoys, Mr. J Hunter and Mr. S Ward were despatched to Corfu. Their mission – smooth operations and report progress. Early news was not good. Opposition was formidable. Though this was not the fault of the Bank, anti-British sentiment was growing.

The Ionian Parliament was dissolved.

Formative months at the Bank had been rough. But, an ingenious solution was to hand. Since the former Legislative Authority enacted an 1837 law for a local bank, which had failed, the two men successfully lobbied that a new local institution should be automatically approved.

On 23 October 1939, The Ionian Bank, having lost the word 'State' during Senate debate, finally emerged as a Joint Stock Company. Interestingly, the name-change did not appear in the Minute Book.

Exclusive rights for note issue were granted for twenty years.

Operations commenced.

All was now in place.

Minutes of 30 December 1839, recorded "resolved that £5000 in British specie be sent out to Corfu by the Packet of the 18 January and that Mr. Ward be authorized to issue drafts on the Bank to the extent of £10,000."

On 2 March 1840, the Bank opened in Corfu. Zante followed on 18 May, Kephalonia by 10 August 1840. 'This Infant Ionian Institution', as it was known in Memoranda of the day between London and the Islands, suffered much petty and vindictive opposition.

Local prejudice, coupled with political unrest, continued. It was hardly surprising that the local Treasurer General was particularly difficult. Until the Bank's launch and despite being a public servant, he had provided private loans and deposits, using the local military safe.

In time, the Bank was able to demonstrate the economic improvements it had brought to the Islands. Opposition evaporated.

However, the Bank still did not have the necessary status in England. Despite the Deed of Settlement, which had permitted operations in the Islands, no such rights existed in Great Britain.

When the Ionian Bank requested an account with Bankers, Messrs. Smith, Payne and Smith, they were formally rebuffed for lack of a proper Charter. An account titled, W. Brown and others, saved their public embarrassment. (Mr. William Brown was a director). Fortunately, a Royal Charter arrived in January 1844.

After the Bank of England, The Ionian Bank's Royal Charter is listed third.

The early years continued to be eventful as the Bank financed growing trade between the Islands and Britain.

Currency fluctuation provided an immediate danger.

With Mexican dollars flowing freely through the Islands, a devaluation in 1844 was met by a Branch Bank Inspector's instruction that "all his payments must be in the sterling value and that discounting any bills care must be taken to make them payable in sterling and to keep as small a stock of Mexican dollars as possible."

Business development continued, with agencies in Patras and Athens to handle the growing ties with Greece. Agents were appointed in Trieste and Venice. Correspondent relationships grew across Europe. Storms beckoned.

Political upheaval reigned in Europe in 1848. Loyal merchants narrowly avoided a run on the Kephalonia branch. A mob attacked Patras, only to be repulsed thanks to HMS Spitfire, Royal Navy. The crop failure in 1851 caused widespread panic in Corfu, wiping out several merchants.

A similar 1857 run and the loss of the currant harvest Zante & Kephalonia were successfully weathered. The Bank's esteem grew. A 20-year licence extension rewarded its care. Under the permit, the Bank Inspector and the Chief Manager had to reside permanently in Corfu. Now the Bank was their own.

Great Britain gave up her sovereignty of the Islands to the Kingdom of Greece in 1864. A new charter changed the Bank to Societe Anonyme and the Government assumed debt responsibilities. Agencies in Athens and Patras developed into formal branches, and in 1873, Athens became HQ.

With the Drachma, as Greece's currency and the Bank still able to issue its own notes, friction was inevitable.

Mr. J Horatio Lloyd resolved the conflict following lengthy and delicate discussions. The Bank would retain its monopoly in the Islands and could expand into Greece, provided the National Bank consented to any new branch where it already had a presence.

Relations flourished and were strengthened to repel the Greek Government's declaration that it would issue notes itself. Within a week, it withdrew.

By granting the Banks increased note-issuing powers and removing obligations to redeem notes in specie, the Government gained a loan of 21 million Drachmas.

Now the Bank's notes were legal tender.

Cautiously the Bank increased its business.

This prudence was to pay dividends when the Greek Government suspended cash payments twice in seven years.

Meanwhile, in Britain, the Bank decided to change to a Joint Stock Company and, in 1883, surrendered its Royal Charter.

The Bank retained its Greek Charter until 1905, though a Special 1880 Law did remove its note-issue monopoly in the Islands. But, for the first time, as a Bank of Issue, the Ionian Bank now equalled the National Bank of Greece.

However, the euphoria looked short-lived. Over the coming years, the National Bank of Greece pressed hard to drive political will to cancel dual-issuing authority.

In 1902, a strong Bank team went to lobby for a renewal of its powers. Opposition was formidable and the venture seemed lost before it commenced.

With the support of Sir Edwin Egerton, British Minister in Greece, and the Bank's overwhelming esteem in the Islands, they won the day against all the odds.

A Royal Decree sealed rights for another 15- year maximum.

Though the Bank did try to sell the issue rights to the National Bank before maturity, a forceful Greek shareholder revolt ensured they remained for the term.

With the impending loss of profitable note-issue, new markets needed to be found. Egypt was chosen. Many Greeks lived there and it was a short southward journey. More importantly, the cotton trade boomed.

A branch opened in Alexandria in 1907. Despite some difficult years, because of the unpredictable reliance on the single crop of cotton, the Bank prospered.

Crop movement and cultivation became specialist areas of investment. Buying and selling formed important income, especially as the Bank pretended to be only an agent. By the 1920s, the Bank was the leading institution handling cotton arrival in Alexandria.

Two world wars tested the Bank.

Although London had frozen all liquid assets, the Bank of England did help offset the withdrawal panic sweeping Greece by honouring due bills.

Throughout the conflict, the Bank helped the Allies in the Balkans and even Turkey's war with Greece had little impact.

In 1922, The Ionian Bank acquired the Guaranty Trust Company of New York's branch in Constantinople.

Even with hopes that when peace returned, it would support business between Turkey and Egypt, seven years later, it closed.

A venture into Cyprus proved much more successful. The Ionian Bank was the first British bank in the country. Five branches quickly spanned the Island.

During 1938, the Bank formed the Ionian Insurance Company and began to acquire Banque Populaire of Greece's 'Big Five'. Germans and Italians had other ideas.

Bank assets were sequestrated.

Banque Populaire became Italian and German insurance companies swallowed the Ionian arm. Many branches were physically damaged.

Although Greek business stood still, the remarkable forethought of the Egyptian venture proved lifesaving. British guarantees for the cotton crop, and huge Allied military spending, surged the market.

Hostilities ceased.

The Ionian ventures were successfully disentangled but the old Drachma was destroyed. Each new Drachma replaced 50 million old ones.

The economy struggled.

By 1952 normality had begun to return, bolstered by the Central Bank of Greece's bold fiscal initiatives.

Today, despite becoming the Ionian and Popular Bank of Greece SA in February 1958, the recent acquisition by Alpha Bank AE, Athens has condemned the name to the mists of time.

The London Branch of the Ionian Bank was bought by Commercial Bank of Greece and opened as a full branch in April 2000.

CHAPTER FOUR

TAIL-LESS CATS & THREE-LEGGED MEN

Becoming the globe's most prudential offshore centre has not been uneventful.

Though tail-less cats and three-legged men inspire mystique, the Isle of Man's financial history is an intriguing reality.

Deprived of intrinsic raw materials, but fortified by 'herrin and spuds' (sea fish and potatoes), Manxmen chose international trade for independent survival.

Manx ships carried the Pilgrim Fathers and helped break the American blockade!

For a time, the Isle was decried as a smugglers' haunt. In 1661 official records show 'a nest of smucklers who glory in their treasons.' Even the local Bishop, in 1742, declared 'the iniquitous trade will hinder the blessing of God from falling upon us.'

The Island had long been a magnet for foreign marauders. Norsemen first recognised the strategic importance for trading and harassing shipping. Adjacent kingdoms, England, Scotland, and Ireland all vied for control.

Now she was in conflict with her current master.

England had granted exclusive charters to companies exploiting her Colonies. The Crown applied taxes to imported goods at home and abroad, including tobacco, tea, silk, salt, wine, and spirits.

Manxmen spotted an opportunity. Provided local dues were met, these products could be re-sold abroad. They began importing, warehousing and re-exporting.

Outraged, the English Government screamed 'smugglers' and applied huge pressure on local officials to stamp out the evil. Manx leaders turned a blind eye. 'Mischief' prevailed.

By 1765, the year of the infamous Stamp Act that sparked the War of Independence, England's patience was exhausted. The Duke of Atholl was pressed to sell all fiscal rights for £70,000.

He did not consult the Manx. They were justifiably furious.

Perhaps, George Quayle, a relation of US Senator Dan Quayle, epitomises the period. Through his forebears' trading success with the Americas and the East, George had a comfortable start to life in 1751.

He soon became popular with local merchants but his family shunned his ambitions in common business. For generations, George's name would not be mentioned at dinner.

In 1802, backed by Major John Taubman, he launched the Island's first bank, The Isle of Man Banking Company. Quayle's notes quickly became known' as good as the Bank of England's.

He closed the bank in 1818. Worthy of standards demanded today, George sold personal property to fully refund depositors.

Many also believe he was an expert 'smuggler'. At Bridge House, in Castletown, now a Museum, his office resembles a stern cabin of Nelson's era. From the deck, with its panoramic view, George monitored traffic, especially the Revenue.

With a secret harbour tunnel, passageways and 'dumb waiters', cargo could be unobtrusively discharged from the dock beneath the building.

Quayle even had a swivelling fireplace concealing a safe. Hidden compartments in chart-lockers and cupboards kept vital documents from prying eyes. Complex locking mechanisms, operated by horsehair cables over remote pulleys, guarded his inconspicuous fortress.

With remarkable foresight, before he died in 1835, he walled-up his small sloop with records, documents, and equipment in her berth beneath the office. Warning his family that doom would descend on anyone who disturbed its fate, 'Peggy' remained in her silt coffin for 100 years until a workman fell through the floor.

Much important history was revealed, including secret plans for a huge barge to carry 30,000 troops for a Napoleonic invasion.

Today, Tynwald, the world's longest-serving continuous Government, steers a booming economy, sustaining independent growth through low, effective taxation.

Bolstered by Moody's and Standard & Poors AAA ratings, the Isle of Man is fully grasping the e-commerce revolution and using her three legs to still run rings around the opposition.

CHAPTER FIVE

THE EURO

Arguably, the most significant change to the world's money markets took place on 1 January 1999. Eleven nations of Europe replaced their currency with the new Euro. The move spelled the end of the Franc and the Mark.

Great Britain, though not joining initially, had not ruled out membership should suitable economic conditions prevail. Ultimately, the step could signal the end of dozens of independent countries and signify the United States of Europe.

Article 105a (1) of the Treaty on European Union, popularly known as the Maastricht Treaty, gave the European Central Bank exclusive right to authorise the issue of banknotes and coin within the participating Member States.

Also established by the Treaty, the European Monetary Institute Council (EMI), formed by the National Central Banks, has two main tasks. Contribute to reaching Stage III of Economic and Monetary Union (EMU), and prepare the European System of Central Banks (ESCB).

December 1995 saw the European Council in Madrid set the framework for banknote and coin production. Euro currency will circulate by January 2002, the exact date announced by the ECB Governing Council before January 1999.

ECOFIN, the European Council of Finance Ministers, entrusted coin production to the Working Group of Mint Directors, consisting of the heads of the National Mints. Eight coins, rising in value from one cent to 2 Euro, will feature in the range. One side of each coin will bear a national design, while the obverse will depict a common pattern.

In June 1997, the Amsterdam European Council endorsed the design for the common side of the coin and invited ECOFIN to adopt the draft Regulation.

Even before the EMI was constituted, long lead times for banknote production led to the committee of the European Central Bank Governors to establish a Working Group on the Printing and Issuing of a European Banknote (BNWG). Comprising Chief Cashiers and General Managers of the NCB printing works, their first decision was to propose a range of seven denominations; 5, 10, 20, 50, 100, 200, and 500.

The EMI Council, on advice from art historians, graphics and marketing experts, selected two themes for a banknote design competition in June 1995; 'Abstract', of the creator's imagination, and 'Ages and Styles of Europe', both bearing the EU flag.

The latter topic represented the architectural history of Europe over distinct periods: Classical, Romanesque, Gothic

Renaissance, Baroque, and Rococo, the Age of Iron and Glass and the 20th Century.

Launched on 12 February 1996, the design competition lasted seven months. After checking for printability and compliance, the NCBs sent the approved designs to a notary in Frankfurt am Main, where a three-digit secret code number replaced authorship identification.

On 20 September 1996, the now anonymous designs were released to the EMI.

A jury of fourteen independent experts from a wide range of disciplines, marketing, art, advertising, etc., representing each EEC country, except Denmark, which had not ratified the Maastricht Treaty, met at the EMI on 26-27 September 1996.

Under the chairmanship of Hanspeter K Scheller, EMI Secretary General, the designs were appraised for creativity, aesthetics, functionality, public perception, avoidance of national bias, and a balance of men and women depicted. Five of each of the two themes provided a shortlist.

Between 7-13 October 1996, Gallup Europe organised a series of focus groups in all EEC countries to evaluate public reaction, consulting 1896 individuals. The results, the jury's appraisal and a technical assessment conducted by the BNWG were submitted to the EMI Council of Governors on 2-3 December 1996.

The winning sketches, in the Ages and Styles of Europe theme, were developed by Robert Kalina of the Oesterreichische Nationalbank. These emphasise windows, gateways and bridges. Blending historical developments, the designs illustrate Europe's common cultural heritage, epitomise the new dawn, and the vision for the future.

On the front, gateways and windows symbolise openness and cooperation. Twelve stars represent the dynamism and harmony of contemporary Europe. Bridges typify European development on the obverse, ranging from pre-Christian constructions to sophisticated suspension bridges, a metaphor for communication among the people of Europe and the world.

Other aspects include the currency name in Latin and Greek, the European flag, the issuing authority initials, BCE, ECB, EZB, EKT, EKP, and the ECB President's signature.

Development of the artwork has been ongoing, turning the winning sketches into sophisticated designs, incorporating the many public and covert security features of a modern banknote.

Dominant colours were chosen by scientific research to assist in recognition. Different note sizes for each denomination with large, bold numerals and tactile features in specific areas were agreed with the European Blind Union to aid the visually impaired.

Modern-day technology offers counterfeiters good results at low cost. To protect banknotes, many security features have been incorporated into the specification.

The paper has fluorescent fibres and both a multitone and barcode watermark, which the forger has difficulty in reproducing. Security thread, intaglio printing and reflective foils are included to help the public.

Several other concealed, machine-readable features enable the NCBs and the note-handling industry to verify authenticity. All aim to detect forgery with a minimum of attention.

Thirteen Member States have printing works. In Belgium, Denmark, Greece, France, Ireland, Italy, Austria and the UK, they are part of the NCB. Finland and Sweden have limited companies wholly owned by their NCB, while Spain has a public company, FNMT.

The Netherlands has a private company, Enschede. Germany's private company is Giesecke & Devrient, Munich and its public company, Bundersdruckerei, Berlin. Portugal buys sheets of partly printed and finishes them itself. Luxembourg sources its banknotes from De La Rue, Gateshead.

These fourteen printers produced nine billion banknotes in 1996, seven billion for domestic use, the rest for issuing authorities outside the EU. With an average life of two years, 12.7 billion banknotes are currently in circulation.

In February 1998, the EMI Council endorsed the final designs together with a full technical specification.

The world awaits the progress of the Euro.

Editor's note: Researched & written 1999.

CHAPTER SIX

AS GOOD AS GOLD - THE HISTORY OF STERLING

Dwarfing the first heartbeats of the infant Euro, England's Pound spans almost an entire millennium.

Even the mighty US Dollar and the vanishing Franc, Mark and Lira can only muster 800 years between them.

Sterling's continuity and prosperity can largely be attributed to three leaders, King Henry VII, Queen Elizabeth I and Lady Margaret Thatcher.

Many have tried to destroy the currency.

Ten centuries ago, the English name 'pound' first appeared. Rooted to Roman Latin, 'pondus' meant 'a weight'. Despite weights devolving into uncla (ounce) and libra (pound) the term survived. Libra's first letter spawned the £ sign.

Pennies created by King Offa of Mercia, an 8th-century monarch better known for his Dyke, would ultimately inspire the Pound.

Nearly 500 years would pass before it would become a gold coin.

Peasants needed little cash. Eggs could be exchanged for Barley. Turnips swapped for milk. Cloth for wood. Barter prevailed.

In rare cases, if cash was essential, a corner could be sliced off a penny. Only wealthy merchants, landowners and the monarchy used money.

When the Vikings discovered Britain's rich lands, money was needed to pay them or repel their advances. A larger unit than a penny became inevitable.

King Alfred's records first mention the Pound.

His grandson, King Athelstan ordered a single national currency, the first in Europe since the Romans.

Even when William the Conqueror vanquished King Harold in 1066 the currency was so well respected that it survived. It supported the Norman's Domesday Book, a thorough register of the nation's assets.

Ordericus Vitalis, a 12-century monk recording Church history wrote the words 'libra sterilensum'. The Pound Sterling was born. Some contend the word emanates from 'esterlin', little star, evident on Norman pennies, which appears in early text as 'starlings'.

In 1108, William's son, King Henry I, decreed that any purveyor of debased silver pennies should be 'castrated and his eyes put out'. Early English silver coins were virtually pure silver, but fraudulent 'skimming and clipping' was increasingly commonplace.

While halving and quartering were routine, deliberate devaluation became a serious crime.

Widespread belief that many silver coins were minted with base metals, to lower production costs and cheat the unwary, convinced people to 'check' coins with cuts and scrapes. Four years later, the resolute monarch decreed that a groove should be cut across the coin's face to prove its content.

Still, the problems continued.

In 1124, the King summoned leading minters. Determined to cease the debased silver pennies, he called them to trial.

Over that Christmas at Winchester, more than one hundred men were separated from their hands and genitalia. They were taken 'one by one and deprived each of the right hand and the testicles beneath', according to documents of the day.

Sadly, little improvement transpired.

In 1279, Edward I initiated strict silver regulations for pennies and introduced farthings (1/4 pennies) and the next year, halfpennies.

As the economy grew, silver groats, worth four pence, arrived to bolster the higher denominations of the shilling, mark and pound.

By 1344, came the 'florin', worth six shillings or 72 pennies and, in 1412, the 'noble' would realise 80 pennies. 1465 witnessed the issue of gold 'ryals' at ten shillings or half a pound.

Foreign coins also gained acceptance to meet the growing shortage of English currency.

An inconspicuous Leicestershire hillside, Bosworth Field, provided the venue for a clash between two mighty medieval armies in 1485. Young Henry Tudor's decisive victory over Richard III ceased years of civil war and sparked economic stability.

Within three years, Henry VII issued the first gold pound coin. Designed by a German, Alexander de Bruchsal, the piece was magnificent – heavy, pure gold.

He encouraged the issue of the gold sovereign and the shilling. Cash usage was further facilitated by denominations of the groat, half groat and penny to the silver angel (1/3 Pound) and ryal (1/2 Pound).

15th century England saw its coinage reported as the 'envy of Europe for its fineness, handsomeness and execution.'

His successor, Henry VIII was not so kind to the currency.

Even vast wealth pillaged from monasteries and churches could not satisfy his lust for war and supplement his lavish court lifestyle.

Soon, the coinage lost its reputation.

New coins were minted in Ireland. These 'harps' paid the soldiers but quickly circulated in England. The Great Debasement continued. Foreign merchants refused English money.

In less than fifty years, his father's great achievement was shattered.

Help was to hand. Queen Elizabeth I, the late King's daughter withdrew the debased money and reissued coins of standard gold and silver measure. Aided by brave and resourceful mariners like Sir Francis Drake, she redressed the balance.

Some historians argue it was little more than state piracy.

In reality, England was a long-term enemy of Spain. These commissioned privateers were authorised to seize foreign treasure at will. Millions poured into the coffers in silver, jewels, art and gold. The value of the pound was again restored.

Throughout the 18th century gold slowly evolved as the underlying choice for coins of high value.

In 1816, Parliament passed The Coinage Act to establish a formal currency system and create the first gold sovereign.

Soon banknotes emerged. These, backed by gold reserves led to the 'Gold Standard.' Britain's banknotes were 'as good as gold' which underpinned her overwhelming economic and monetary superiority.

Unlike earlier wars, which had actually helped the Pound, the First World War generated economic chaos. For the first time in centuries, war challenged the Pound's indomitable position.

In 1933, Britain was forced to drop The Gold Standard. The USA seized firm industrial control to catapult the Dollar as the pre-eminent international currency.

The Second World War only added to the Pound's misery.

Closer European ties in 1971 saw Decimalisation herald an end to tradition with the death of 20 Shillings and 240 Pence to the Pound.

During the 1980s, Lady Margaret Thatcher brilliantly transformed Britain's sick industrial base to restore the respect, trust and confidence the Pound enjoys today.

No longer gold, today's coin is a blend of copper, zinc and nickel weighing a mere 9.5 grams. Will it endure?

Or, as history reveals, will another weak and indulgent custodian write a final chapter?

C H A P T E R S E V E N

SCRIPOPHILY

Imagine, you could acquire millions of pounds in international investments for relatively nothing!

A pyramid scam? The dubious sale of a national monument? No, Scripophily.

Old share and bond collecting is arguably the world's fastest-growing hobby and investment opportunity. Attracting 120,000 collectors in twenty years, denounced financial documents are seeing a valuable renaissance.

Henry Wells and William Fargo could not have possibly conceived that routine American Express papers, signed 150 years ago, would today realise over £1000 each.

Scripophily has ensured that.

In 1978, the blossoming hobby needed a name. The Times ran a competition. Scrip, short for subscription receipt, a debt acknowledgement loosely meaning shares, was fused with Philos, Greek for loving.

The love of shares was born.

Enthusiasts have their own favourite subjects. Some relish ornate illustrations and artistic content. Others appreciate the explosive development of commerce, roads, railways, bridges, canals, banking dynasties, shipping lines, states and nations.

Certificates range from postcard to opened broadsheet newspaper size, which many collectors proudly display on the walls of their homes and offices. Securities make good taking points and unusual gifts for friends, colleagues and clients.

Scripophilists argue that shares and bonds have greater historical significance than paintings, stamps or banknotes. Per square inch, they offer better value for money.

THE GREEN SHOOTS OF MONEY · 49

Sometimes, the attraction is a signature, made famous by the passage of time. A Standard oil founder's share, signed by John D Rockefeller, can change hands for over $60,000.

Russian loan certificates, though generally in poor condition, but hand-signed by Nathan Mayer Rothschild in 1822, will fetch £70-£100. The forerunner to Getty Oil, Mission Development Company bearing John Paul Getty's autograph, can be yours for under £10.

Modern shares are not entirely ignored. Redundant copies of Walt Disney or Planet Hollywood stock with the facsimile signatures of Stallone, Arnie, and Willis already fetch £65.

However, history fascinates many. Railroad companies that interlaced the frontier towns of America, funded by $1000 certificates redeemable in gold coin, Britain's Stockton & Darlington Railway Company, The Confederacy.

Other collectors favour themes, insurance, hotels, animals, cars, aircraft, mining, or entertainment. The list is endless. Some choose countries like Brazil, Costa Rica, Mexico, Egypt, Romania, China, and Russia.

Major international bond launches were printed in Great Britain.

Bradbury Wilkinson & Co Limited and Waterlow & Sons Limited, now part of the De La Rue Group, which prints UK banknotes, and remains the globe's premier securities' producer, were selected for these large, colourful and intricate products.

Though the vast majority of certificates are discharged or reneged, some could yet be fulfilled. China and Russia are still at the forefront of defaulted national debt.

Owners remain hopeful that eventually their trust will be repaid.

Only a decade ago, with the help of the Bank of England, UK holders of eighty-year-old defunct Russian debt received partial payments.

Researching a bond or share increases interest and adds value when you come to sell. Bonds can relate intrigue, power-lust, spectacular collapse, fraud, and even murder. They reflect the aspirations and, in some cases, the miserable failure of enterprises and governments.

Documents usually have a story to tell. Canada is a rich source of the world's precious minerals, the Klondike Gold Rush, immortalised by Charlie Chaplin, an early instance.

Harsh weather and topography caused many failures. Fred Stark Pearson, director of the San Antonio Land and Irrigation Company Limited and his associate Alfred Lowenstein, who also built electric tramways in Brazil, Mexico and Spain, were famous entrepreneurs of the time.

Pearson drowned in 1915 when a German submarine torpedoed the Lusitania.

Mysteriously, Lowenstein fell from his own aircraft when travelling to France in 1928. Krueger & Toll, a Swedish company, which once dominated the world's match business, was finished by rumours of fraud.

Where do you find them? Phillips and Christies now hold three specific auctions a year. International dealers will offer you comprehensive illustrated catalogues and webpages.

Thirty international auction houses prove the rising trend. Regular monthly postal and live auctions take place in Germany, the USA, Switzerland, and Belgium.

The UK has a dedicated promotion group, the International Bond & Share Society, founded in 1978, which issues a quarterly magazine with a free bulletin board and an annual directory of members.

Corresponding clubs and societies encourage collectors in Europe, Australia, South Africa, the USA and Canada. Occasionally, a valuable bond is unearthed when sorting a deceased relative's cupboards. Junk shops, curio arcades, car-boot sales, and deed boxes all reveal interesting finds.

Now that the borders of China and Russia are open, caches should emerge. Meanwhile, the German government has a large stockpile, which it is considering releasing to the public.

As companies rely on computerised records, original historical chronicles will increase in rarity, and ultimately, in value. Unfortunately, recent EU data-protection legislation could hasten the destruction of irreplaceable investment paperwork.

Remember, shares and certificates were working documents, made to be handled. They can show serious signs of wear. But beware, the ravages of time may not necessarily detract from a share's worth, if only poor samples are known to exist.

Always try to obtain the best example.

Formal classification has evolved from the banknote and stamp fields. Mint, uncirculated, very fine, cancelled are all identifiable terms, but rarity and popularity have an overriding influence.

Despite huge public offerings, many Russian certificates are rare because of their turbulent history. However, not many people collect them, so they are inexpensive.

On the other hand, American railroad shares are hugely popular internationally and can command a disproportionate price.

Storing certificates carefully is essential. Many have been folded for storage in the past and you must take care when preserving them. The folds, while being a weak point, add to the character and opening them out should reduce further deterioration. Try to keep your collection flat in a dry secure place.

Mice, spiders and mould can play havoc with prices! Protective acid-free tissue covers are best. Artists' satchels can be useful for storage and transport.

If you decide to display your prized possessions, make sure that your framer uses acid-free and UV stabilized glass. Never hang your showpiece in direct sunlight, it will fade.

THE GREEN SHOOTS OF MONEY · 55

A good practise when building your collection is to record the source, price and any identifying marks. Colour copies of a valuable piece can be a wise investment. Make sure that your domestic insurance covers your collection, particularly when you buy expensive items.

Your Scripophily collection can be acquired modestly, swapping and selling unwanted items as you develop a particular area of interest. It will increase in value, but experts would advise buying what you enjoy, rather than for investment.

Next time you visit that old aunt or uncle, ask if they have any redundant shares, you might make their retirement even happier.

BIBLIOGRAPHY

Clapham, J. (1944). *The Bank of England a History*. Cambridge: Cambridge University Press.

Houseman, L. (1968). The House That Thomas Built. London: Chatto & Windus.

Ionian Bank. (1953). *The Ionian Bank - A History*. London: The Ionian Bank.

Moncrief-Scott, I. (2000). *As Good As Gold - History of Pound Sterling*. York: Appleton.

Moncrief-Scott, I. (2000). *Currants, Olives & Cotton*. York: Appleton.

Moncrief-Scott, I. (1999). D*e La Rue Straw Hats to Global Securities*. York: Appleton.

Moncrief-Scott, I. (1999). E*uro - History & Development*. York: Appleton.

Moncrief-Scott, I. (1999). *Scripophily - Historic Bond & Share Collecting*. York: Appleton.

Moncrief-Scott, I. (2000). *Tail-less Cats & Three-Legged Men*. York: Appleton.

Moncrief-Scott, I. (2000). *The Eternal Old Lady - Bank of England - History & Development*. York: Appleton.

Richards, R.D. (1934) *The First 50 Years of The Bank of England (1694–1744)*. Leiden: Nijhoff.

Saw, R. (1944). *The Bank of England 1694-1944*. London: Harrap.

OTHER BOOKS BY THE AUTHOR

As Good As Gold - History of Pound Sterling. ISBN 0-9534818-4-0

De La Rue Straw Hats to Global Securities. ISBN 0- 9534818-2-4

Euro History & Development. ISBN 0-9534818-1-6

Holidays 2000 – A Time Capsule. ISBN 0-9534818-7-5

Negotiate to Win! - The Introductory Edition. ISBN 0-9534818-6-7

Start Any Business (Print). ISBN 9781903467008
Start Any Business (eBook). ISBN 9781903467015

Scripophily - Historic Bond & Share Collecting. ISBN 0-9534818-5-9

The Eternal Old Lady - Bank of England. ISBN 0-9534818-3-2

The Green Shoots of Money (eBook). ISBN 9781903467114

The Hitmen - Part One. ISBN 0-9534818-8-3

FORTHCOMING BOOKS BY THE AUTHOR

As Good As Gold (Print). ISBN 9781903467039
As Good As Gold (eBook). ISBN 9781903467121

Currants, Olives & Cotton (Print). ISBN 9781903467077
Currants, Olives & Cotton (eBook). ISBN 9781903467169

De La Rue (Print). ISBN 9781903467046
De La Rue (eBook). ISBN 9781903467138

Euro (Print). ISBN 9781903467053
Euro (eBook). ISBN 9781903467145

Scripophily (Print). ISBN 9781903467084
Scripophily (eBook). ISBN 9781903467176

Tail-less Cats & Three-legged Men (Print). ISBN 9781903467091
Tail-less Cats & Three-legged Men (eBook). ISBN 9781903467183

The Eternal Old Lady (Print). ISBN 9781903467060
The Eternal Old Lady (eBook). ISBN 9781903467152

ABOUT THE AUTHOR

Ian Moncrief-Scott has over fifty years of broad business experience, mostly gained at international level, based in the UK.

As a former senior executive for a global publishing and information technology company headquartered in the USA, he has contributed to numerous client-facing procurement and outsourcing initiatives worldwide.

Ian has created and participated in numerous small businesses in the UK, Isle of Man and elsewhere.

He has also represented the Isle of Man Government Department for Enterprise in several of its business support schemes. Ian designed and delivered extensive training for its Micro Business Grant Scheme.

In recognition of his long-term service to the Department, Ian was nominated for The Queen's Award for Enterprise Promotion and awarded an official Certificate of Recognition in 2018.

Throughout his career, he has maintained an active interest in start-ups, especially those involving the financial sector.

At the turn of the millennium, several of the articles written by Ian that form this short work were originally published by the Museum of American Financial History (now the Museum of American Finance).

www.ingramcontent.com/pod-product-compliance
Lightning Source LLC
Chambersburg PA
CBHW041959080526
44588CB00021B/2799